MW01290189

JOHN HENRY NEWMAN

From a drawing by G. Richmond

in the possession of H. E. Wilberforce, Esq.

THE DREAM OF

GERONTIUS

BY

CARDINAL NEWMAN

CBy Students' Edition

CBY PUBLISHING 2018

MIDDLESEX

TABLE OF CONTENTS

INTRODUCTION

BY

MAURICE FRANCIS EGAN, A.M., LL.D.

PROFESSOR OF ENGLISH LANGUAGE AND LITERATURE IN THE CATHOLIC

UNIVERSITY OF AMERICA, WASHINGTON, D. C.

A s a rule, when Cardinal Newman's poetry is mentioned, people think of "The Pillar of the Cloud," better known as "Lead, Kindly Light." This lyric is only one of the many beautiful poems written by an author whose fame as a writer of the finest modern prose in the English language has eclipsed his reputation as a poet. Nevertheless, he wrote a very great poem, "The Dream of Gerontius"—a poem which the intellectual world admires more and more every year, and which yields its best only after careful study and consideration. It has been described as a metrical meditation on death. It is more than that; it is the realization by means of a loving heart and a poetic imagination of the state of a just soul after death,—Gerontius typifying not the soul of a particular person imagined by Cardinal Newman, but your soul, my soul, any soul which may be fortunate enough to satisfy the judging and merciful God. No poet has ever presented the condition of the soul, as made known by the theology of the Catholic Church, so forcibly and appealingly as Cardinal Newman. The poem is filled with intense white light, and the soul on earth sees itself as it will be at the moment before its death; as it will be when, strengthened by the last sacraments and upborne by the prayers of its friends, it approaches the bar of judgment. Separated from the body until the day of the Resurrection, when it shall be united to that glorified body, it is not sundered by death from the love of those who have loved it on earth. Gerontius about to be judged feels that he must fail

> "And drop from out the universal frame
>
> Into that shapeless, scopeless, blank abyss,
>
> That utter nothingness"

from which the soul came, and, in its depths of fear, it pleads silently that its friends in Christ may pray for it. The dread of annihilation is upon it; it fears "the great deep"[1] to which it goes. And, in the agony of its rending from the beloved body, it thinks — for it can no longer speak — of the horror of nothingness. All its physical supports are gone. Its eyes are darkening and glazing; its feet motionless and cold; its arms and hands rigid. To those in the sick-room the body once so beautiful,

> "from the graced decorum of the hair
>
> Ev'n to the tingling sweet
>
> Soles of the simple, earth-confiding feet,"[2]

is now white as white marble and as lifeless. But the soul is not dead, though the earthly parts of the body appear to be, and it hears the prayers of the Church for the dying as the supreme moment of its departure from the body is at hand. Some of these prayers, translated from the Latin, the author puts into the mouths of the assistants. They have all the refreshing strength that the Church gives; they represent the supplication of millions of devout souls bound to this dying brother in the communion of saints. The soul gains new strength from these prayers; it arouses

---

[1] From Merlin's song in Tennyson's "Coming of Arthur."
[2] Coventry Patmore's "Ode to the Body."

itself; sees God through the ruin of the world, and wills to be wholly His. The assistants by the bedside redouble their supplications in the sacred words of the Litany for the Dying, which Cardinal Newman again interprets in English verse, though the Litany is in the Latin tongue. Again, the soul gains strength for a moment, and calls, in the universal speech of the Church, for strength, and that, "out of the depths,"[3] the holy God might save it. Then it uses its will to believe, and within itself asserts the creed of the Church, which is musically interpreted by the poet:

> "Firmly I believe and truly
>
> God is Three, and God is One,
>
> And I next acknowledge duly
>
> Manhood taken by the Son."

The moment of agony, the moment of the realization of the soul that it is alone, bereft of its support, is terrible but short. In the "Inferno" of Dante, with all its objective horrors, there are no lines so terrible as these, which show the spirit naked, wild with horror and dismay:

> "And worse and worse,
>
> Some bodily form of ill
>
> Floats on the wind, with many a loathsome curse
>
> Tainting the hallowed air, and laughs and flaps
>
> Its hideous wings."

We can imagine the scene in the room in which Gerontius is dying. The priest, in his surplice and violet stole, has sprinkled the chamber and the persons present with holy water, using the form of the cross, and has said the *Asperges*:

---

[3] From the Psalm, "De profundis clamavi ad te, Domine." — "Out of the depths have I cried to Thee, O Lord."

"Thou shall sprinkle me with hyssop, and I shall be cleansed: Thou shalt wash me, and I shall be made whiter than snow."

Gerontius has kissed the crucifix, and it is still before him. In the glow of the lighted candle the "Litany for the Dying" is recited by the priest and the "assistants," that is to say, all in the room who will pray. The passing of the soul may not have occupied a second, as we reckon time, and yet, as "The Dream of Gerontius" suggests, the soul, sensitive and vital, may live through what might seem to be a hundred years. As soon as it appears that the soul has departed, the priest says:

"Subvenite, Sancti Dei, occurrite Angeli Domini, Suscipientes animam ejus, Offerentes eam in conspectu Altissimi."[4]

This prayer dwells last in the ears of Gerontius. He has slept for a moment, refreshed by the Church, and he awakes to find himself free.

"I had a dream; yes: some one softly said

'He's gone,' and then a sigh went round the room,

And then I surely heard a priestly voice

Cry 'Subvenite,' and they knelt in prayer."[5]

The soul, borne forward on its way to the Judge, hears the song of its Guardian Angel, whose work is done. As the soul proceeds, the voices of the demons are heard; they express the pride of those who defy God. They cry out:

---

[4] "Come to his assistance, ye saints of God; come forth to meet him, ye angels of the Lord: Receiving his soul: Offering it in the sight of the Most High."

[5] This passage in "The Dream of Gerontius" calls to mind Tennyson's lines in "The Princess":
"Ah, sad and strange, as in dark summer dawns
The earliest pipe of half-awakened birds
To dying ears, when unto dying eyes
The casement slowly grows a glimmering square."

"Virtue and vice,

A knave's pretence,

'Tis all the same."

The soul wonders why it cannot move hand or foot, and the angel says:

"Nor hast thou now extension, with its parts

Correlative, — long habit cozens thee, —

Nor power to move thyself, nor limbs to move."

So infinitesimal has the time been since the soul left the body that the "Subvenite" is not yet finished when the soul is at the very throne of Judgment:

"I hear the voices that I left on earth."

The angel answers:

"It is the voice of friends around thy bed

Who say the 'Subvenite' with the priest."

The angel of the Agony supplicates for the soul, as for its brother, and then the eager spirit darts forward alone to the feet of God. Gerontius is judged; he passes lovingly to Purgatory. His Guardian Angel says:

"And ye great powers,

Angels of Purgatory, receive from me

My charge, a precious soul, until the day

When, from all bond and forfeiture released,

I shall reclaim it for the courts of light."

Waiting until he shall enter into the full glory of the Lord, Gerontius is left by the poet. This soul knows now what it did not know on earth, — what the real happiness of Heaven is; "it measures the distance which separates itself from this happiness.

It understands how infinite this distance is, through its own fault. It suffers terribly. Its sorrow grows with its love, as it loves God more and more with all the fibres of its being; it is drawn by vital and mighty bonds towards the object of its love, but each bond is broken by the weight of its faults, which like a mass of lead hold it down."[6]

There can be no question as to the correspondence of the teaching of Cardinal Newman with the theology of the Catholic Church. Dante is put by Raphael, in the famous picture, the Disputà, among the Doctors of the Church, and the author of "The Dream of Gerontius" would have merited a similar honor even if he had never been created[7] a Cardinal.

For advanced students interested in the study of literature a comparative reading of "The Dream of Gerontius" with the "Purgatorio" of Dante, Book III, Milton's "Paradise Lost," Rossetti's "The Blessed Damosel," and Tennyson's "In Memoriam" would be very interesting and profitable, provided this is done always with reference to the exact teaching of the Church. For exalted purity, for terseness and beauty of expression, for musical cadences, "The Dream of Gerontius" stands first among the few great poems that depict the life after death. "In Memoriam" is made up of human yearnings, of faith, of doubt. It never passes beyond "the bar" of death. Milton's "Paradise" is one of angels rather than men, and Rossetti's poem is only a reflection of earth. In Dante's "Purgatorio" the splendor seems to be so great that the appeal to the individual heart is lost, but the oftener we read "The Dream of Gerontius," the more its power and beauty and peace grow upon us.

The story of General Charles George Gordon, "Chinese Gordon," one of the heroes of the nineteenth century, has passed

---

[6] La Psychologie du Purgatoire (The Psychology of Purgatory): Abbé Chollet, Doctor of Theology at Lille.

[7] The Holy Father "creates" Cardinals, he does not appoint them.

into history, and every enthusiastic boy or girl ought to know it by heart. Gordon was the type of the valiant soldier who carried the love and fear of God everywhere. He, besieged by pagan hordes, died, in 1884, the death of a martyr to duty. This man was only one of those who found consolation in "The Dream of Gerontius" at the very hour of death. General Gordon's copy of the poem—a small duodecimo—was presented to the late Mr. Frank Power, correspondent of the London *Times*. The latter sent it home to his sister in Dublin. Deep pencil-marks had been drawn under lines all bearing on death and prayer. For instance: "Pray for me, O my friends"; "'Tis death, O loving friends, your prayers,—'tis he"; "So pray for me, my friends, who have not strength to pray"; "Use well the interval"; "Prepare to meet thy God"; "Now that the hour is come, my fear is fled." Later Power met the fate of a hero. The last words that Gordon underlined before he gave him the book were:

"Farewell, but not forever, brother dear;

Be brave and patient on thy bed of sorrow."

The metre in "The Dream of Gerontius" changes with the thought, and it is always appropriate to it. The solemn movement of the opening lines gives the typical music, which is varied lyrically. As an example of exquisite musical variety on a firm basis of unity the poem is admirable. The level of "Lead, Kindly Light" is reached many times in the expression of the highest faith and love, and in musical quality the famous hymn is even surpassed by

"Take me away, and in the lowest deep

There let me be."

Why Cardinal Newman should have presented the experience of a soul after death as a "dream" we can imagine from his habitual caution in dealing with all subjects of importance. He has the boldness of neither Dante nor Milton, and he will not present the poetical experience of a man, at such a vitally sacred moment, as an actual fact; he is too reverential for that, and he calls it a "Dream." In a letter written in answer to an inquiry as to the meaning of the lines in "The Pillar of the Cloud,"

> "And with the morn those angel faces smile
>
> Which I have loved long since, and lost awhile," —

he says, quoting Keble, that poets are "not bound to be critics or to give a sense to what they had written,"[8] and he adds that "there must be a statute of limitations, or it would be quite a tyranny, if in an art which is the expression not of truth but of imagination and sentiment, one were obliged to stand an examination on the transient state of mind which came upon one when homesick, or seasick, or in any other way sensitive or excited."

It is well to take a great poem like this without too much inquiry or analysis. If the author's intention is not evident in his poem, either he has failed to be clear, or he is consciously obscure, or we are incapable of appreciating his work. The first and second defects do not appear in "The Dream of Gerontius." The third, let us trust, does not exist in us. The notes, few in number, are intended to explain only what is not obvious.

In his "Recollections" Aubrey De Vere says: "'The Dream of Gerontius,' as Newman informed me, owed its preservation to an accident. He had written it on a sudden impulse, put it aside and forgotten it. The editor of a magazine" — it appeared in *The Month*, of London, 1865, in two parts — "wrote to him asking for a contribution. He looked into all his pigeon-holes and found nothing theological; but, in answering his correspondent, he added that he had come upon some verses which, if, as editor, he

---

[8] Catholic Life and Letters by Cardinal Newman; with Notes on the Oxford Movement and its Men: — John Oldcastle (Mr. Wilfred Meynell). To which work the editor is under obligation for important parts of the appended chronology.

cared to have, were at his command. The wise editor did care, and they were published at once."

R. H. Hutton, writing of Cardinal Newman, speaks in this way of "The Dream of Gerontius": "Before the Vatican disputes and shortly after the controversy with Canon Kingsley, Newman had written a poem of which he himself thought so little that it was, as I have heard, consigned or doomed to the waste-basket.... Some friend who had an eye for true poetry rescued it, and was the means, therefore, of preserving to the world one of the most unique and original poems of the present century, as well as that one of all of them which is, in every sense, the least in sympathy with the temper of the present century.... None of his writings engraves more vividly on his readers the significance of the intensely practical convictions which shaped his career. And especially it impresses on us one of the great secrets of his influence. For Newman has been a sign to this generation that unless there is a great deal of the loneliness of death in life, there can hardly be much of the higher equanimity of life in death. To my mind 'The Dream of Gerontius' is the poem of a man to whom the vision of the Christian revelation has at all times been more real, more potent to influence action, and more powerful to preoccupy the imagination than all worldly interests put together." (R. H. Hutton, "Cardinal Newman.")

The song of the soul in "The Dream of Gerontius" has sometimes been compared with "The Pillar of the Cloud"—a sacred lyric which is a household canticle wherever the English language is spoken. It is often misquoted, a fourth stanza having been added to it. This is the authorized version:

"Lead, kindly Light, amid the encircling gloom

Lead Thou me on!

The night is dark, and I am far from home—

Lead Thou me on!

Keep Thou my feet; I do not ask to see

The distant scene—one step enough for me.

"I was not ever thus, nor prayed that Thou

Shouldst lead me on.

I loved to choose my path, but now

Lead Thou me on.

I loved the garish day, and, spite of fears,

Pride ruled my will; remember not past years.

"So long Thy power hath blest me, sure it still

Will lead me on,

O'er moor and fen, o'er crag and torrent till

The night is gone;

And with the morn those angel faces smile

Which I have loved long since, and lost awhile."

In the "Apologia Pro Vita Sua" Dr. Newman wrote: "We"—Mr. Hurrell Froude, brother of the historian James Anthony Froude, being the other person—"set out in December 1832. It was during this expedition that my verses which are in the 'Apostolica' were written—a few, indeed, before it, but not more than one or two of them after it. At Whitechurch, while waiting for the down mail to Falmouth, I wrote the verses about 'My Guardian Angel' which begin with these words:

"'Are these the tracks of some unearthly friend?'"

It must be remembered that John Henry Newman had not yet entered the Catholic Church. It is strange that he should at this time have held the belief in a ministering spirit which is so marked in "The Dream of Gerontius."

In the sextette of this sonnet he says:

"Were I Christ's own, then fitly might I call

That vision real; for to the thoughtful mind

That walks with Him He half reveals His face;

But when on earth-stained souls such tokens fall,

These dare not claim as theirs what there they find,

Yet, not all hopeless, eye His boundless grace."

This vision, he says, "which haunted me, — the vision is more or less brought out in the whole series of compositions." "Gerontius" itself is more a "vision" than a "dream."

"The Pillar of the Cloud" was written in an orange-boat. "We were becalmed a whole week in the Straits of Bonifaccio. Then it was," he says in the "Apologia" — the finest model of modern English prose extant — "that I wrote 'Lead, Kindly Light,' which has since become well known. I was writing verses the whole time of my passage."

The "vision" of which he speaks he saw everywhere, and all his poems seem, in one way or other, to contain hints of the great poem to come; for there can be no doubt that "The Dream of Gerontius" is the culmination of his poetical moods. One cannot open any of his prose works without finding allusions to these eternal truths made so clear through the processes of the soul of a normal old man, — our young readers will please look up the derivation of Gerontius[9], which is from the Greek, — but it is in his poems that we discover easily the germs of his poetical masterpiece. Even in the poems he loved we note the constant dwelling on the main theme of "The Dream" — Eternity. In 1889

---

[9] γερων — οντος.

Cardinal Newman was very ill. During his convalescence he asked that Faber's "Eternal Years"[10] should be sung to him with musical accompaniment. He said that he would like to hear it when he came to die. It is a poem of sixteen stanzas, to be found in Faber's "Hymns." It begins:

"How shalt thou bear the cross that now

So dread a weight appears?

Keep quietly to God, and think

Upon the eternal years.

Austerity is little help,

Although it sometimes cheers;

Thine oil of gladness is the thought

Of the eternal years."

"Novissima hora est!" Gerontius exclaims, "and I fain would sleep." He is thinking of the eternal hours and years in this last hour on earth.

At sea, in June, 1833, Newman had written some verses called "Hora Novissima":

"Whene'er goes forth Thy dread command,

And my last hour is nigh,

Lord, grant me in a Christian land,

As I was born, to die.

"I pray not, Lord, that friends may be,

---

10 The text of which is reproduced on page 82.

Or kindred, standing by, —

Choice blessing! which I leave to Thee

To grant me or deny.

"But let my falling limbs beneath

My Mother's smile recline,

And prayers sustain my laboring breath

From out her sacred shrine.

"And let the cross beside my bed

In its dread presence rest;

And let the absolving words be said

To ease a laden breast.

"Thou, Lord, where'er we lie, canst aid;

But He who taught His own

To live as one, will not upbraid

The dread to die alone."

The death of Gerontius was Newman's ideal Christian death, and Gerontius does not die alone; he is upborne, refreshed by the prayers of his friends. Of Newman's sacred songs, "The Pillar of the Cloud" is, as we know, put first by some critics. And yet for musical diction, for sweetness and all the beauty of artistic technique, the song of the soul in "The Dream" equals if not surpasses it.

"Take me away, and in the lowest deep,

There let me be,

And there in hope the lone night-watches keep,

Told out for me."

In "Verses on Various Occasions" there is the picture of the resigned souls expecting the Blessed Vision. "Waiting for the Morning" was written at Oxford, 1835. It begins:

"They are at rest;

We may not stir the heaven of their repose

With loud-voiced grief, or passionate request,

Or selfish plaints for those

Who in the mountain grots of Eden lie,

And hear the fourfold river as it passes by."

By "Eden" Newman symbolized the paradise — the resting-place of souls — of the fourfold rivers. Here they patiently abide,

"And soothing sounds

Blend with the neighboring waters as they glide;

Posted along the haunted garden's bounds

Angelic forms abide,

Echoing as words of watch, o'er lawn and grove,

The verses of that hymn which seraphs chant above."

The fulness of higher meditation and knowledge is in the triumphant song of the Soul, but "Waiting for the Morning" contains its suggestion, just as "The Lady of Shalott" by Lord Tennyson contains the germ of the exquisite "Elaine."

The dedication of "The Dream of Gerontius" reads, in English: "To the Most Beloved Brother, John Joseph Gordon, Priest of the Order of St. Philip de Neri, whose soul is in the Place of Refreshment[11]. All Souls' Day, 1865."

The Rev. John Joseph Gordon, of the Oratory, was very dear to Newman, and his death was a great blow to him. But of all the Oratorians, the Cardinal especially loved Father Ambrose St. John, whose name he accentuates on the last page of the "Apologia." Father St. John, who was of the Gordon family, died in 1875, and Newman suffered what he held to be his saddest bereavement. Ambrose St. John had been with him at Littlemore. Writing to Mr. Dering of the death of Father Ambrose St. John, he said: "I never had so great a loss. He had been my life under God for twenty-two years." The dread of dying alone and the deep affection for friends — an affection that reaches the throne of God by prayer — tinge the whole structure of "The Dream." They are part of Newman himself.

Cardinal Newman died at Edgbaston Oratory, August 11, 1890; he was buried, at his own request, in the grave with Father Ambrose St. John. "'The Dream of Gerontius' was composed in great grief after the death of a dear friend."

A careful study of "The Dream of Gerontius" will show how musical it is, and how delicately the music of the verse changes with the themes. The form of poetry, as we know, approaches music. If a poem is not musical in expression, its metres fail of producing the effect they are intended to produce. So musical is "The Dream of Gerontius" and so capable of being treated by the musicians, that various composers suggested the making of an oratorio of it. Dr. Elgar has done it. "An Ursuline," in *The Catholic World*, for June, 1903, says: "Dr. Elgar, when a child, sat Sunday after Sunday in the organ-loft of St. George's Roman Catholic Church, Worcester, England, where his father

---

[11] The word "refrigerium" was used for "refreshment," "rest" in the epitaphs of the early Latin Christians.

had been organist for the long period of thirty-seven years. Subtly the spirit of the grand old church music was instilled into the boy." Of "The Dream" Dr. Elgar said: "The poem has been soaking in my mind for at least eight years. All that time I had been gradually assimilating the thoughts of the author into my musical promptings." In 1889 a copy of the poem, with the markings made by General Gordon, was presented to Dr. Elgar as a wedding gift. The markings of the heroic and devout Gordon especially interested him. The reading of this little book helped to make Dr. Elgar's fame, which is based solely on his masterpiece, the oratorio performed in London on June 6, 1903, in Westminster Cathedral. Richard Strauss is looked on by musicians as the master of what is called "tone-color" — a perfect harmony between the tone of the instrument and the music arranged for it. But the German and English critics declare that in "The Dream of Gerontius" Dr. Elgar has surpassed Richard Strauss. "The Demons' Chorus," says The *Pall Mall Gazette*, "may be regarded as one of the last words of musical audacity." For the study of the music we suggest Dr. Jaeger's Analysis, printed by Novello in London and New York. Mr. Theodore Thomas, speaking of Dr. Elgar's "Dream of Gerontius," said that it is the most important oratorio of recent times, not excepting Brahms' Requiem. "'Gerontius,'" he added, "is a lofty work, and, from a technical point of view, more masterly than Brahms ever dreamed of. It is by far the most important and satisfying modern work written for voices and orchestra."

It is understood that Cardinal Newman himself suggested that his poem should be set to music. The delicacy of his ear as to sounds is shown by the changes of the verse-music, — which is made up of accent, pause, and rhythm, — to fit the varying feeling of the work. If the student will scan the lines and reduce them to musical expression, — leaving out, of course, the quality of pitch, he can easily corroborate this.

Jĕsu, Mărĭă, Ī ăm nēar tŏ dēath,
And Thŏu ărt cāllĭng mē.

This is in two-beat rhythm:

      The first syllable of "Jesu" is the anacrusis; the measure of the metre begins with the first accent. Whether this system of verse-notation or that of the usual scansion be followed, the meaning of the changing forms will be made plain. The system of verse-notation will be found more satisfactory in the metrical study of the poem. The second form of primary rhythm — that based on three beats in the measure — is effectively used. We find it in the Song of the Demons:

Lŏw-bŏrn clōds
Ŏf brŭte eārth,
Thĕy ăspīre,—

JOHN HENRY NEWMAN

Born in the city of London, February 21, 1801, son of Mr. John Newman (of the banking firm of Ramsbottom, Newman & Co.) and of Jemima Fourdrinier, his wife.

Went at an early age to Dr. Nicholas's school at Ealing, to the head of which he rapidly rose. Thence to Trinity College, Oxford, graduating in 1820.

In 1823 was elected to a Fellowship at Oriel.

In 1824 took Anglican orders and became curate of St. Clements, Oxford.

In 1828 was appointed vicar of St. Mary the Virgin, Oxford, with the outlying chaplaincy of Littlemore.

In 1832 finished *History of the Arians* and went abroad. Made acquaintance with Dr. Wiseman in Rome; seized with fever in Sicily, but said, "I shall not die—I have a work to do in England"; returning homewards in an orange-boat bound for Marseilles, and within sight of Garibaldi's home at Caprera, wrote "Lead, Kindly Light."

On July 13, 1833, the Sunday after his return home, the Oxford movement was begun by Keble's sermon on National Apostasy. The issue of *Tracts for the Times* immediately followed; and in 1843 Mr. Newman published a volume of *Parochial Sermons*, to be followed by *University Sermons* and *Sermons on Holy Days*.

In 1841 the Vice-Chancellor and heads of houses at Oxford censured Mr. Newman's Tract XC.

In 1843 he resigned St. Mary's.

On October 9, 1845, was received into the Catholic Church at Littlemore by Father Dominic.

On November 1, 1845, was confirmed at Oscott by Cardinal Wiseman.

On October 28, 1846, arrived in Rome, and, after a short period of study, was ordained priest.

On Christmas Eve, 1847, he returned to England from Rome, to found the community of St. Philip de Neri.

In January, 1849, part of the Oratorian Community settled in Birmingham.

In 1849 took up temporary residence at Bilston, to nurse the poor during a visitation of cholera.

In April, 1849, founded the London Oratory, with Father Faber as rector.

On June 21, 1852, the case of Achilli against Dr. Newman came on for trial before Lord Campbell, and, after several days' duration, resulted in a verdict of "guilty," Dr. Newman being unjustly sentenced to a fine and mulcted in enormous costs. The Rev. John Joseph Gordon, to whom "The Dream of Gerontius" is dedicated, was of great assistance to Newman at this time.

In 1854 went to Dublin as rector of the newly founded Irish Catholic University, but resigned that post in 1858, and subsequently established a boys' school at Birmingham.

In 1864 Charles Kingsley made charges of untruthfulness against the Catholic clergy, which led to the writing of the *Apologia Pro Vita Sua*.

In December, 1877, was elected an Honorary Fellow of Trinity College, Oxford.

In 1865 he printed "The Dream of Gerontius."

In 1879 created Cardinal Deacon of the Holy Roman Church by Leo XIII.

On Monday, August 11, 1890, died at the Oratory, Edgbaston, Birmingham, England.

THE DREAM OF GERONTIUS

PHASE I.

GERONTIUS[12]

Jesu, Maria—I am near to death[13],

And Thou art calling me; I know it now—

Not by the token of this faltering breath,

This chill at heart, this dampness on my brow,

---

[12] As suggested in the Introduction, the musical character of the verse of "The Dream of Gerontius" is brought out more and more by careful study of the changes of the meaning of the poem and their expression. "The Dream" is a series of lyrics,—each lyric voicing its own feeling and sensitively tuned to that feeling. According to the scansion most in use in English, the first supplicating lyric may be classed as in pentameter iambic. Gerontius is yet in the body, and the rime, used solemnly, marks a difference—which has a delicate symbolism—between his utterances in the body and his utterances when his soul has left the body. What we call blank verse is used by the Spirit—rime disappears, but the rhythm remains the same. Using verse-notation, we find five accented notes in each line, if we consider the lines at all. There are two quarter-notes in each bar, which may be written as

[13] Gerontius dreams that he is dying. He has not strength to pray. He hears the persons near his bed praying for him, in the language prescribed by the Church, "The Litany for the Dying." The three opening invocations are in Greek, "Kyrie Eleison" ("Lord, have mercy"), "Christe Eleison" ("Christ, have mercy"), "Kyrie Eleison" ("Lord, have mercy"). The next invocation in the Litany is "Sancta Maria, Ora pro eo," which Cardinal Newman translates into English. With the exception of the first three and the last two invocations, the Litany is in Latin. The Litany is too long for the purpose of the poem, and the author has translated into English some of the invocations that would naturally strike the "fainting soul." "Be merciful" ("Propitius esto"), the assistants continue, still using parts of the Litany as versified by Cardinal Newman.

(Jesu, have mercy! Mary, pray for me!) —

'Tis this new feeling, never felt before,

(Be with me, Lord, in my extremity!)

That I am going, that I am no more.

'Tis this strange innermost abandonment,

(Lover of souls! great God! I look to Thee,)

This emptying out of each constituent

And natural force, by which I come to be.

Pray for me, O my friends; a visitant

Is knocking his dire summons at my door,

The like of whom, to scare me and to daunt,

Has never, never come to me before;

'Tis death, — O loving friends, your prayers! — 'tis he!...

As though my very being had given way,

As though I was no more a substance now,

And could fall back on nought to be my stay,

(Help, loving Lord! Thou my sole Refuge, Thou,)

And turn no whither, but must needs decay

And drop from out the universal frame

Into that shapeless, scopeless, blank abyss,

That utter nothingness, of which I came:

This is it that has come to pass in me;

O horror! this it is, my dearest, this;

So pray for me, my friends, who have not strength to pray.

ASSISTANTS

Kyrie eleïson[14], Christe eleïson, Kyrie eleïson.

Holy Mary, pray for him.

All holy Angels, pray for him.

Choirs of the righteous, pray for him.

Holy Abraham, pray for him.

St. John Baptist, St. Joseph, pray for him.

St. Peter, St. Paul, St. Andrew, St. John,

All Apostles, all Evangelists, pray for him.

All holy Disciples of the Lord, pray for him.

All holy Innocents, pray for him.

All holy Martyrs, all holy Confessors,

All holy Hermits, all holy Virgins,

All ye Saints of God, pray for him.

GERONTIUS

Rouse thee[15], my fainting soul, and play the man;

    And through such waning span

    Of life and thought as still has to be trod,

---

[14] *"Kyrie Eleïson,"* etc. The poet has retained the sound-form used in the Prayer-books, and he shows his musical taste by not changing it.

[15] *"Rouse thee,"* etc. Gerontius concentrates all his vitality. The effect is of nervous energy. The time is quickened and alternately slowed.

Prepare to meet thy God.

And while the storm of that bewilderment

Is for a season spent,

And, ere afresh the ruin on thee fall,

Use well the interval.

ASSISTANTS

Be merciful[16], be gracious; spare him, Lord.

Be merciful, be gracious; Lord, deliver him.

From the sins that are past;

From Thy frown and Thine ire;

From the perils of dying;

From any complying

With sin, or denying

His God, or relying

On self, at the last;

From the nethermost fire

---

[16] *"Be merciful,"* etc. The Assistants begin with the solemn chant of the Church, and change to the supplication of anxious human hearts:

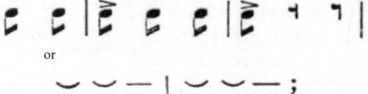

or

From all that is evil;

From power of the devil;

Thy servant deliver,

For once and for ever.

By Thy birth, and by Thy Cross,

Rescue him from endless loss;

By Thy death and burial,

Save him from a final fall;

By Thy rising from the tomb,

By Thy mounting up above,

By the Spirit's gracious love,

Save him in the day of doom.

Sanctus fortis, Sanctus Deus[17],

De profundis oro te,

Miserere, Judex meus,

Parce mihi, Domine[18].

Firmly I believe and truly

---

[17] *"Sanctus fortis, Sanctus Deus,"* etc. This is the ecstasy of faith, hope, and love. It is three Acts in one, rapidly and forcibly expressed. The energy and strength of self-forgetfulness fail when he, still in the body, sighs:

"I can no more; for now it comes again," —

Note the musical effect of

"And, crueller still,

A fierce and restless fright begins to fill

The mansion of my soul. And, worse and worse,

Some bodily form of ill."

The pauses after "ill" express horror and weakness, —

[18] Holy Strong One, Holy God,
From the depth I pray to Thee.
Mercy, O my Judge, for me;
Spare me, Lord.

In the Proper for the season of Good Friday the passage which suggested this reads, in Greek and Latin:

1st choir. Agios O Theos (O Holy God).
2d choir. Sanctus Deus (O Holy God).
1st choir. Agios Ischyros (O Holy Strong One).
2d choir. Sanctus Fortis (O Holy Strong One).

God is Three, and God is One;

And I next acknowledge duly

Manhood taken by the Son.

And I trust and hope most fully

In that Manhood crucified;

And each thought and deed unruly

Do to death, as He has died.

Simply to His grace and wholly

Light and life and strength belong,

And I love, supremely, solely,

Him the holy, Him the strong.

Sanctus fortis, Sanctus Deus,

De profundis oro te,

Miserere, Judex meus,

Parce mihi, Domine.

And I hold in veneration,

For the love of Him alone,

Holy Church, as His creation,

And her teachings, as His own.

And I take with joy whatever

Now besets me, pain or fear,

And with a strong will I sever

All the ties which bind me here.

Adoration aye be given

> With and through the angelic host,

To the God of earth and heaven,

> Father, Son, and Holy Ghost.

Sanctus fortis, Sanctus Deus,

> De profundis oro te,

Miserere, Judex meus,

> Mortis in discrimine[19].

I can no more; for now it comes again,

That sense of ruin, which is worse than pain,

That masterful negation and collapse

Of all that makes me man; as though I bent

Over the dizzy brink

Of some sheer infinite descent;

Or worse, as though

Down, down for ever I was falling through

The solid framework of created things,

And needs must sink and sink

Into the vast abyss. And, crueller still,

A fierce and restless fright begins to fill

The mansion of my soul. And, worse and worse,

---

[19] Death dissolves me.

Some bodily form of ill

Floats on the wind, with many a loathsome curse

Tainting the hallowed air, and laughs, and flaps

Its hideous wings,

And makes me wild with horror and dismay.

O Jesu, help! pray for me, Mary, pray!

Some angel, Jesu! such as came to Thee

In Thine own agony....

Mary, pray for me. Joseph, pray for me.

Mary, pray for me.

ASSISTANTS

Rescue him, O Lord, in this his evil hour,

As of old so many by Thy gracious power: — (Amen.)

Enoch and Elias from the common doom; (Amen.)

Noe from the waters in a saving home; (Amen.)[20]

Abraham from th' abounding guilt of Heathenesse; (Amen.)

Job from all his multiform and fell distress; (Amen.)

Isaac, when his father's knife was raised to slay; (Amen.)

Lot from burning Sodom on its judgment-day; (Amen.)

Moses from the land of bondage and despair; (Amen.)

---

[20] "Rescue him, O Lord," etc. The solemn chant again. Note the difference in metre between this and the "Novissima hora est; and I fain would sleep. The pain has wearied me." Note the ardor of the Priest's "Proficiscere, anima Christiana," etc.

Daniel from the hungry lions in their lair; (Amen.)

And the Children Three amid the furnace-flame; (Amen.)

Chaste Susanna from the slander and the shame; (Amen.)

David from Golia and the wrath of Saul; (Amen.)

And the two Apostles from their prison-thrall; (Amen.)

Thecla from her torments; (Amen.)

— so, to show Thy power,

Rescue this Thy servant in his evil hour.

GERONTIUS

Novissima hora est[21]; and I fain would sleep,

The pain has wearied me.... Into Thy hands,

O Lord, into Thy hands....

THE PRIEST

Proficiscere, anima Christiana, de hoc mundo[22]!

Go forth upon thy journey, Christian soul!

Go from this world! Go, in the name of God,

The omnipotent Father, who created thee!

Go, in the name of Jesus Christ, our Lord,

---

[21] The final hour is here. "Into Thy hands." The whole of this prayer for the dying is: "Into Thy hands, O Lord, I commend my spirit. O Lord Jesus, receive my spirit. Holy Mary, pray for me. O Mary, Mother of grace, Mother of mercy, do thou protect me from the enemy and receive me at the hour of death."

[22] "Go forth, O Christian soul, from this world." These words begin the prayer of the priest, recited while the soul is departing from the body. It is paraphrased in English by the Cardinal.

Son of the living God, who bled for thee!

Go, in the Name of the Holy Spirit, who

Hath been poured out on thee! Go, in the name

Of Angels and Archangels; in the name

Of Thrones and Dominations; in the name

Of Princedoms and of Powers; and in the name

Of Cherubim and Seraphim, go forth!

Go, in the name of Patriarchs and Prophets;

And of Apostles and Evangelists,

Of Martyrs and Confessors; in the name

Of holy Monks and Hermits; in the name

Of holy Virgins; and all Saints of God,

Both men and women, go! Go on thy course;

And may thy place to-day be found in peace,

And may thy dwelling be the Holy Mount

Of Sion: — in the Name of Christ, our Lord.

PHASE II.

SOUL OF GERONTIUS

I went to sleep; and now I am refreshed[23].

A strange refreshment: for I feel in me

An inexpressive lightness, and a sense

Of freedom, as I were at length myself,

And ne'er had been before. How still it is!

I hear no more the busy beat of time,

No, nor my fluttering breath, nor struggling pulse;

Nor does one moment differ from the next.

I had a dream; yes: — some one softly said

"He's gone"; and then a sigh went round the room.

And then I surely heard a priestly voice

Cry "Subvenite"; and they knelt in prayer.

I seem to hear him still; but thin and low,

And fainter and more faint the accents come,

As at an ever-widening interval.

Ah! whence is this? What is this severance?

This silence pours a solitariness

Into the very essence of my soul;

---

[23] "I went to sleep," etc. The soul of Gerontius has left the body:

And the deep rest, so soothing and so sweet,

Hath something too of sternness and of pain,

For it drives back my thoughts upon their spring

By a strange introversion, and perforce

I now begin to feed upon myself,

Because I have nought else to feed upon.

Am I alive or dead? I am not dead,

But in the body still; for I possess

A sort of confidence which clings to me,

That each particular organ holds its place

As heretofore, combining with the rest

Into one symmetry, that wraps me round,

And makes me man; and surely I could move,

Did I but will it, every part of me.

And yet I cannot to my sense bring home,

By very trial, that I have the power.

'Tis strange; I cannot stir a hand or foot,

I cannot make my fingers or my lips

By mutual pressure witness each to each,

Nor by the eyelid's instantaneous stroke

Assure myself I have a body still.

Nor do I know my very attitude,

Nor if I stand, or lie, or sit, or kneel.

So much I know, not knowing how I know,

That the vast universe, where I have dwelt,

Is quitting me, or I am quitting it.

Or I or it is rushing on the wings

Of light or lightning on an onward course,

And we e'en now are million miles apart.

Yet ... is this peremptory severance

Wrought out in lengthening measurements of space,

Which grow and multiply by speed and time?

Or am I traversing infinity

By endless subdivision, hurrying back

From finite towards infinitesimal,

Thus dying out of the expansive world?

Another marvel[24]: someone has me fast

Within his ample palm; 'tis not a grasp

Such as they use on earth, but all around

---

[24] "Another marvel." According to the teaching of the Catholic Church, each soul is given at its birth in charge of a Guardian Angel. It is this angel that sings, "My work is done." "Alleluia" is from two Hebrew words united by a hyphen. It means "Praise the Lord." St. John in the Apocalypse says that he heard the angels singing it in heaven. It occurs in the last five Psalms and in Tobias.

Over the surface of my subtle being,

As though I were a sphere, and capable

To be accosted thus, a uniform

And gentle pressure tells me I am not

Self-moving, but borne forward on my way.

And hark! I hear a singing; yet in sooth

I cannot of that music rightly say

Whether I hear or touch or taste the tones.

Oh what a heart-subduing melody!

ANGEL

My work is done[25],

    My task is o'er,

        And so I come,

        Taking it home,

For the crown is won,

      Alleluia.

    For evermore.

---

[25] "My work is done,
My task is o'er,"
is expressed with a joyous movement, —

My Father gave

    In charge to me

        This child of earth

        E'en from its birth,

To serve and save,

        Alleluia,

    And saved is he.

This child of clay

    To me was given,

        To rear and train

        By sorrow and pain

In the narrow way,

        Alleluia,

    From earth to heaven.

SOUL

It is a member of that family

Of wondrous beings, who, ere the worlds were made,

Millions of ages back, have stood around

The throne of God: — he never has known sin;

But through those cycles all but infinite,

Has had a strong and pure celestial life,

And born to gaze on th' unveiled face of God

And drank from the eternal Fount of truth,

And served Him with a keen ecstatic love.

Hark! he begins again.

ANGEL

O Lord, how wonderful in depth and height,

      But most in man, how wonderful Thou art!

With what a love, what soft persuasive might

      Victorious o'er the stubborn fleshly heart

    Thy tale complete of saints Thou dost provide

    To fill the thrones which angels lost through pride!

He lay a grovelling babe upon the ground,

      Polluted in the blood of his first sire,

With his whole essence shattered and unsound,

      And, coiled around his heart, a demon dire,

    Which was not of his nature, but had skill

    To bind and form his opening mind to ill.

Then was I sent from heaven to set right

      The balance in his soul of truth and sin,

And I have waged a long relentless fight,

      Resolved that death-environed spirit to win,

    Which from its fallen state, when all was lost,

~ 45 ~

Had been repurchased at so dread a cost.

Oh, what a shifting parti-coloured scene

    Of hope and fear, of triumph and dismay,

Of recklessness and penitence, has been

    The history of that dreary, lifelong fray!

And oh the grace to nerve him and to lead,

How patient, prompt, and lavish at his need!

O man, strange composite of heaven and earth[26]!

    Majesty dwarfed to baseness! fragrant flower

Running to poisonous seed! and seeming worth

    Cloking corruption! weakness mastering power!

Who never art so near to crime and shame,

As when thou hast achieved some deed of name; —

How should ethereal natures comprehend

    A thing made up of spirit and of clay,

Were we not tasked to nurse it and to tend,

    Linked one to one throughout its mortal day?

More than the Seraph in his height of place,

---

[26] Compare the thought in "Hamlet" — Act II, Scene II. — "What a piece of work is man!"

The Angel-guardian knows and loves the ransomed race.

SOUL

Now know I surely that I am at length

Out of the body: had I part with earth,

I never could have drunk those accents in,

And not have worshipped as a god the voice

That was so musical; but now I am

So whole of heart, so calm, so self-possessed,

With such a full content, and with a sense

So apprehensive and discriminant,

As no temptation can intoxicate.

Nor have I even terror at the thought

That I am clasped by such a saintliness.

ANGEL

All praise to Him, at whose sublime decree

The last are first, the first become the last;

By whom the suppliant prisoner is set free,

By whom proud first-borns from their thrones are cast,

Who raises Mary to be Queen of heaven,

While Lucifer is left, condemned and unforgiven.

PHASE III.

SOUL

I will address him. Mighty one, my Lord,

My Guardian Spirit, all hail!

ANGEL

All hail, my child!

My child and brother, hail! what wouldest thou?

SOUL

I would have nothing but to speak with thee

For speaking's sake. I wish to hold with thee

Conscious communion; though I fain would know

A maze of things, were it but meet to ask,

And not a curiousness.

ANGEL

You cannot now

Cherish a wish which ought not to be wished.

SOUL

Then I will speak. I ever had believed

That on the moment when the struggling soul

Quitted its mortal case, forthwith it fell

Under the awful Presence of its God,

There to be judged and sent to its own place.

What lets me now from going to my Lord?

ANGEL

Thou art not let; but with extremest speed

Art hurrying to the Just and Holy Judge:

For scarcely art thou disembodied yet.

Divide a moment, as men measure time,

Into its million-million-millionth part,

Yet even less than that the interval

Since thou didst leave the body; and the priest

Cried "Subvenite[27]," and they fell to prayer;

Nay, scarcely yet have they begun to pray.

For spirits and men by different standards mete

The less and greater in the flow of time.

By sun and moon, primeval ordinances —

By stars which rise and set harmoniously —

By the recurring seasons, and the swing,

This way and that, of the suspended rod

Precise and punctual, men divide the hours,

---

[27] When the soul has departed, the priest says the prayer beginning "Subvenite, Sancti Dei; occurrite Angeli Domini," etc. ("Come to his assistance, ye saints of God," etc.).

Equal, continuous, for their common use.

Not so with us in the immaterial world;

But intervals in their succession

Are measured by the living thought alone,

And grow or wane with its intensity.

And time is not a common property;

But what is long is short, and swift is slow,

And near is distant, as received and grasped

By this mind and by that, and every one

Is standard of his own chronology.

And memory lacks its natural resting-points

Of years, and centuries, and periods.

It is thy very energy of thought

Which keeps thee from thy God.

SOUL

Dear Angel, say,

Why have I now no fear at meeting Him?

Along my earthly life, the thought of death

And judgment was to me most terrible.

I had it aye before me, and I saw

The Judge severe e'en in the crucifix.

Now that the hour is come, my fear is fled;

And at this balance of my destiny,

Now close upon me, I can forward look

With a serenest joy.

ANGEL

It is because

Then thou didst fear, that now thou dost not fear.

Thou hast forestalled the agony, and so

For thee the bitterness of death is past.

Also, because already in thy soul

The judgment is begun. That day of doom,

One and the same for the collected world —

That solemn consummation for all flesh,

Is, in the case of each, anticipate

Upon his death; and, as the last great day

In the particular judgment is rehearsed,

So now too, ere thou comest to the Throne,

A presage falls upon thee, as a ray

Straight from the Judge, expressive of thy lot.

That calm and joy uprising in thy soul

Is first-fruit to thee of thy recompense,

And heaven begun.

PHASE IV.

SOUL

　　　　　　　But hark! upon my sense

Comes a fierce hubbub, which would make me fear,

Could I be frighted.

ANGEL

　　　　　　　We are now arrived

Close on the judgment court; that sullen howl

Is from the demons who assemble there.

It is the middle region, where of old

Satan appeared among the sons of God,

To cast his jibes and scoffs at holy Job.

So now his legions throng the vestibule,

Hungry and wild, to claim their property,

And gather souls for hell. Hist to their cry.

SOUL

How sour and how uncouth a dissonance!

Low-born clods[28]

    Of brute earth,

        They aspire

To become gods,

    By a new birth,

And an extra grace,

    And a score of merits.

        As if aught

Could stand in place

        Of the high thought,

      And the glance of fire

Of the great spirits,

The powers blest,

    The lords by right,

      The primal owners,

        Of the proud dwelling

And realm of light, —

Dispossessed,

---

[28] *"Low-born clods,"* etc. The most marked change comes here. The solemnity and sweetness of the soul and the angel's music — their *leit-motif* — is easily discernible. Now come dissonances and discords, — the rapidity of jangled cymbals struck in scorn. The phrase "chucked down" has been censured as "inelegant." Its meaning and sound accord exactly with the spirit of the demoniac chorus.

Aside thrust,

                    Chucked down,

    By the sheer might

        Of a despot's will,

                  Of a tyrant's frown.

          Who after expelling

          Their hosts, gave,

       Triumphant still,

And still unjust,

                  Each forfeit crown

        To psalm-droners,

        And canting groaners,

          To every slave,

        And pious cheat,

          And crawling knave,

Who licked the dust

           Under his feet.

ANGEL

It is the restless panting of their being;

Like beasts of prey, who, caged within their bars,

In a deep hideous purring have their life,

And an incessant pacing to and fro.

DEMONS

The mind bold

And independent,

The purpose free,

So we are told,

Must not think

To have the ascendant.

What's a saint?

One whose breath

Doth the air taint

Before his death;

A bundle of bones,

Which fools adore,

Ha! ha!

When life is o'er,

Which rattle and stink,

E'en in the flesh.

We cry his pardon!

No flesh hath he;

Ha! ha!

For it hath died,

'Tis crucified

Day by day,

Afresh, afresh,

Ha! ha!

That holy clay,

Ha! ha!

This gains guerdon,

So priestlings prate,

Ha! ha!

Before the Judge,

And pleads and atones

For spite and grudge,

And bigot mood,

And envy and hate,

And greed of blood.

SOUL

How impotent they are! and yet on earth

They have repute for wondrous power and skill;

And books describe, how that the very face

Of the Evil One, if seen, would have a force

Even to freeze the blood, and choke the life

Of him who saw it.

ANGEL

In thy trial-state

Thou hadst a traitor nestling close at home,

Connatural, who with the powers of hell

Was leagued, and of thy senses kept the keys,

And to that deadliest foe unlocked thy heart.

And therefore is it, in respect to man,

Those fallen ones show so majestical.

But, when some child of grace, angel or saint,

Pure and upright in his integrity

Of nature, meets the demons on their raid,

They scud away as cowards from the fight.

Nay, oft hath holy hermit in his cell,

Not yet disburdened of mortality,

Mocked at their threats and warlike overtures;

Or, dying, when they swarmed, like flies, around,

Defied them, and departed to his Judge.

DEMONS

Virtue and vice,

A knave's pretence.

'Tis all the same;

Ha! ha!

Dread of hell-fire,

Of the venomous flame,

A coward's plea.

Give him his price,

                Saint though he be,

Ha! ha!

      From shrewd good sense

            He'll slave for hire;

        Ha! ha!

           And does but aspire

To the heaven above

          With sordid aim,

And not from love.

         Ha! ha!

SOUL

I see not those false spirits; shall I see

My dearest Master, when I reach His throne;

Or hear, at least, His awful judgment-word

With personal intonation, as I now

Hear thee, not see thee, Angel? Hitherto

All has been darkness since I left the earth;

Shall I remain thus sight bereft all through

My penance time? If so, how comes it then

That I have hearing still, and taste, and touch,

Yet not a glimmer of that princely sense

Which binds ideas in one, and makes them live?

Nor touch, nor taste, nor hearing hast thou now;

Thou livest in a world of signs and types,

The presentations of most holy truths,

Living and strong, which now encompass thee.

A disembodied soul, thou hast by right

No converse with aught else beside thyself;

But, lest so stern a solitude should load

And break thy being, in mercy are vouchsafed

Some lower measures of perception,

Which seem to thee, as though through channels brought,

Through ear, or nerves, or palate, which are gone.

And thou art wrapped and swathed around in dreams,

Dreams that are true, yet enigmatical;

For the belongings of thy present state,

Save through such symbols, come not home to thee.

And thus thou tell'st of space, and time, and size,

Of fragrant, solid, bitter, musical,

Of fire, and of refreshment after fire;

As (let me use similitude of earth,

To aid thee in the knowledge thou dost ask) —

As ice which blisters may be said to burn.

Nor hast thou now extension[29], with its parts

Correlative, — long habit cozens thee, —

Nor power to move thyself, nor limbs to move.

Hast thou not heard of those, who, after loss

Of hand or foot, still cried that they had pains

In hand or foot, as though they had it still?

So is it now with thee, who hast not lost

Thy hand or foot, but all which made up man;

So will it be, until the joyous day

Of resurrection, when thou wilt regain

All thou hast lost, new-made and glorified.

How, even now, the consummated Saints

See God in heaven, I may not explicate.

Meanwhile let it suffice thee to possess

Such means of converse as are granted thee,

Though, till that Beatific Vision thou art blind;

For e'en thy purgatory, which comes like fire,

Is fire without its light.

SOUL

His will be done!

---

[29] "Extension," "the position of parts outside parts." See p. 366, General Metaphysics, by John Rickaby, S.J., Manuals of Catholic Philosophy.

I am not worthy e'er to see again

The face of day; far less His countenance

Who is the very sun. Nathless, in life,

When I looked forward to my purgatory,

It ever was my solace to believe,

That, ere I plunged amid th' avenging flame,

I had one sight of Him to strengthen me.

ANGEL

Nor rash nor vain is that presentiment;

Yes, — for one moment thou shalt see thy Lord.

Thus will it be: what time thou art arraigned

Before the dread tribunal, and thy lot

Is cast for ever, should it be to sit

On His right hand among His pure elect,

Then sight, or that which to the soul is sight,

As by a lightning-flash, will come to thee,

And thou shalt see, amid the dark profound,

Whom thy soul loveth, and would fain approach, —

One moment; but thou knowest not, my child,

What thou dost ask: that sight of the Most Fair

Will gladden thee, but it will pierce thee too.

SOUL

Thou speakest darkly, Angel! and an awe

Falls on me, and a fear lest I be rash.

ANGEL

There was a mortal, who is now above

In the mid glory: he, when near to die,

Was given communion with the Crucified, —

Such, that the Master's very wounds were stamped

Upon his flesh[30]; and, from the agony

Which thrilled through body and soul in that embrace

Learn that the flame of the Everlasting Love

Doth burn ere it transform....

---

[30] St. Francis d'Assisi. In 1224, while on Mount Alvernus, keeping a fast of forty days in honor of St. Michael, a seraph appeared and marked the hands, feet, and right side of St. Francis with the five wounds of Our Lord's Passion.

Phase V.

... Hark to those sounds!

They come of tender beings angelical,

Least and most childlike of the sons of God.

First Choir of Angelicals

Praise to the Holiest in the height[31],

   And in the depth be praise:

In all His words most wonderful;

   Most sure in all His ways!

To us His elder race He gave

   To battle and to win,

Without the chastisement of pain,

   Without the soil of sin.

---

[31] "Praise to the Holiest in the height." A movement associated by English readers with the hymn particularly:

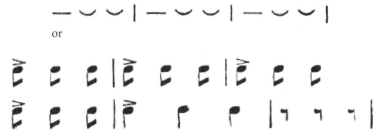

~ 63 ~

The younger son He willed to be

    A marvel in his birth:

Spirit and flesh his parents were;

    His home was heaven and earth.

The Eternal blessed His child, and armed,

    And sent him hence afar,

To serve as champion in the field

    Of elemental war.

To be His Viceroy in the world

    Of matter, and of sense;

Upon the frontier, towards the foe,

    A resolute defence.

ANGEL

We now have passed the gate, and are within

The House of Judgment; and whereas on earth

Temples and palaces are formed of parts

Costly and rare, but all material,

So in the world of spirits nought is found,

To mould withal and form into a whole,

But what is immaterial; and thus

The smallest portions of this edifice,

Cornice, or frieze, or balustrade, or stair,

The very pavement is made up of life —

Of holy, blessed, and immortal beings,

Who hymn their Maker's praise continually.

SECOND CHOIR OF ANGELICALS

Praise to the Holiest in the height,

    And in the depth be praise:

In all His words most wonderful;

    Most sure in all His ways!

Woe to thee, man! for he was found

    A recreant in the fight;

And lost his heritage of heaven,

    And fellowship with light.

Above him now the angry sky,

    Around the tempest's din;

Who once had angels for his friends,

    Had but the brutes for kin.

O man! a savage kindred they;

    To flee that monster brood

He scaled the seaside cave, and clomb

The giants of the wood.

With now a fear, and now a hope,
    With aids which chance supplied,
From youth to eld, from sire to son,
    He lived, and toiled, and died.

He dreed[32] his penance age by age;
    And step by step began
Slowly to doff his savage garb,
    And be again a man.

And quickened by the Almighty's breath,
    And chastened by His rod,
And taught by Angel-visitings,
    At length he sought his God:

And learned to call upon His name,
    And in His faith create
A household and a fatherland,
    A city and a state.

---

[32] "Dreed," from the old English verb "dreogan," to suffer.

Glory to Him who from the mire,

  In patient length of days,

Elaborated into life

  A people to His praise!

SOUL

The sound is like the rushing of the wind —

The Summer wind among the lofty pines;

Swelling an rd dying, echoing round about,

Now here, now distant, wild and beautiful;

While, scattered from the branches it has stirred,

Descend ecstatic odours.

THIRD CHOIR OF ANGELICALS

Praise to the Holiest in the height,

  And in the depth be praise:

In all His words most wonderful;

  Most sure in all His ways!

The Angels, as beseemingly

  To spirit-kind was given,

At once were tried and perfected,

  And took their seats in heaven.

For them no twilight or eclipse;

    No growth and no decay:

'Twas hopeless, all-ingulfing night,

    Or beatific day.

But to the younger race there rose

    A hope upon its fall;

And slowly, surely, gracefully,

    The morning dawned on all.

And ages, opening out, divide

    The precious and the base,

And from the hard and sullen mass,

    Mature the heirs of grace.

O man! albeit the quickening ray,

    Lit from his second birth,

Makes him at length what once he was,

    And heaven grows out of earth;

Yet still between that earth and heaven —

    His journey and his goal —

A double agony awaits

His body and his soul.

A double debt he has to pay —
    The forfeit of his sins,
The chill of death is past, and now
    The penance-fire begins.

Glory to Him, who evermore
    By truth and justice reigns;
Who tears the soul from out its case,
    And burns away its stains!

ANGEL

They sing of thy approaching agony,
Which thou so eagerly didst question of:
It is the face of the Incarnate God
Shall smite thee with that keen and subtle pain;
And yet the memory which it leaves will be
A sovereign febrifuge to heal the wound;
And yet withal it will the wound provoke,
And aggravate and widen it the more.

SOUL

Thou speakest mysteries; still methinks I know

To disengage the tangle of thy words:

Yet rather would I hear thy angel voice,

Than for myself be thy interpreter.

ANGEL

When then — if such thy lot — thou seest thy Judge,

The sight of Him will kindle in thy heart,

All tender, gracious, reverential thoughts.

Thou wilt be sick with love, and yearn for Him,

And feel as though thou couldst but pity Him,

That one so sweet should e'er have placed Himself

At disadvantage such, as to be used

So vilely by a being so vile as thee.

There is a pleading in His pensive eyes

Will pierce thee to the quick, and trouble thee.

And thou wilt hate and loathe thyself; for, though

Now sinless, thou wilt feel that thou hast sinned,

As never thou didst feel; and wilt desire

To slink away, and hide thee from His sight

And yet wilt have a longing aye to dwell

Within the beauty of His countenance.

And these two pains, so counter and so keen, —

The longing for Him, when thou seest Him not;

The shame of self at thought of seeing Him, —

Will be thy veriest, sharpest purgatory.

SOUL

My soul is in my hand: I have no fear, —
In His dear might prepared for weal or woe.
But hark! a grand mysterious harmony:
It floods me, like the deep and solemn sound
Of many waters.

ANGEL

We have gained the stairs
Which rise towards the Presence-chamber; there
A band of mighty Angels keep the way
On either side, and hymn the Incarnate God.

ANGELS OF THE SACRED STAIR

Father, whose goodness none can know, but they
Who see Thee face to face,
By man hath come the infinite display
Of Thy victorious grace;
But fallen man — the creature of a day —
Skills not that love to trace.
It needs, to tell the triumph Thou hast wrought,
An Angel's deathless fire, an Angel's reach of thought.

It needs that very Angel, who with awe,

    Amid the garden shade,

The great Creator in His sickness saw,

    Soothed by a creature's aid,

And agonised, as victim of the Law

    Which He Himself had made;

For who can praise Him in His depth and height,

But he who saw Him reel amid that solitary fight?

SOUL

Hark! for the lintels of the presence-gate

Are vibrating and echoing back the strain.

FOURTH CHOIR OF ANGELICALS

Praise to the Holiest in the height,

    And in the depth be praise:

In all His words most wonderful;

    Most sure in all His ways!

The foe blasphemed the Holy Lord,

    As if He reckoned ill,

In that He placed His puppet man

    The frontier place to fill.

For even in his best estate,

    With amplest gifts endued,

A sorry sentinel was he,

    A being of flesh and blood.

As though a thing, who for his help

    Must needs possess a wife,

Could cope with those proud rebel hosts,

    Who had angelic life.

And when, by blandishment of Eve,

    That earth-born Adam fell,

He shrieked in triumph, and he cried,

    "A sorry sentinel;

The Maker by His word is bound,

    Escape or cure is none;

He must abandon to his doom,

    And slay His darling son."

ANGEL

And now the threshold, as we traverse it,

Utters aloud its glad responsive chant.

Praise to the Holiest in the height,

    And in the depth be praise:

In all His words most wonderful;

    Most sure in all His ways!

O loving wisdom of our God!

    When all was sin and shame,

A second Adam to the fight

    And to the rescue came.

O wisest love! that flesh and blood

    Which did in Adam fail,

Should strive afresh against the foe,

    Should strive and should prevail;

And that a higher gift than grace

    Should flesh and blood refine,

God's Presence and His very Self,

    And Essence all divine.

O generous love! that He who smote

    In man for man the foe,

The double agony in man

    For man should undergo;

And in the garden secretly,

    And on the cross on high,

Should teach His brethren and inspire

    To suffer and to die.

PHASE VI.

ANGEL

Thy judgment now is near, for we are come

Into the veiled presence of our God.

SOUL

I hear the voices that I left on earth.

ANGEL

It is the voice of friends around thy bed,

Who say the "Subvenite" with the priest.

Hither the echoes come; before the Throne

Stands the great Angel of the Agony,

The same who strengthened Him, what time He knelt

Lone in the garden shade, bedewed with blood.

That Angel best can plead with Him for all

Tormented souls, the dying and the dead.

Jesu! by that shuddering dread which fell on Thee;

Jesu! by that cold dismay which sickened Thee;

Jesu! by that pang of heart which thrilled in Thee;

Jesu! by that mount of sins which crippled Thee;

Jesu! by that sense of guilt which stifled Thee;

Jesu! by that innocence which girdled Thee;

Jesu! by that sanctity which reigned in Thee;

Jesu! by that Godhead which was one with Thee;

Jesu! spare these souls which are so dear to Thee,

Who in prison, calm and patient, wait for Thee;

Hasten, Lord, their hour, and bid them come to Thee,

To that glorious Home, where they shall ever gaze on Thee.

SOUL

I go before my Judge. Ah!...

ANGEL

... Praise to His Name!

The eager spirit has darted from my hold,

And, with the intemperate energy of love,

Flies to the dear feet of Emmanuel;

But, ere it reach them, the keen sanctity,

---

[33] *"Angel of the Agony."* Note the solemn and pathetic rhythm effect.

Which with its effluence, like a glory, clothes

And circles round the Crucified, has seized,

And scorched, and shrivelled it; and now it lies

Passive and still before the awful Throne.

O happy, suffering soul! for it is safe,

Consumed, yet quickened, by the glance of God.

SOUL

Take me away, and in the lowest deep[34]

　　　There let me be,

And there in hope the lone night-watches keep,

　　　Told out for me.

There, motionless and happy in my pain,

　　　Lone, not forlorn, —

There will I sing my sad perpetual strain,

　　　Until the morn.

There will I sing, and soothe my stricken breast,

　　　Which ne'er can cease

To throb, and pine, and languish, till possest

　　　Of its Sole Peace.

---

[34] *"Take me away, and in the lowest deep,*
There let me be," etc.
The catalexis — pause — is finely used here:

There will I sing my absent Lord and Love: —

Take me away,

That sooner I may rise, and go above,

And see Him in the truth of everlasting day.

PHASE VII.

ANGEL

Now let the golden prison ope its gates,

Making sweet music, as each fold revolves

Upon its ready hinge. And ye great powers,

Angels of Purgatory, receive from me

My charge, a precious soul, until the day,

When, from all bond and forfeiture released,

I shall reclaim it for the courts of light.

SOULS IN PURGATORY[35]

1. Lord, Thou hast been our refuge: in every generation;

2. Before the hills were born, and the world was: from age to age Thou art God.

---

[35] This appeal is paraphrased by the author from the Psalms. The words at the end are translated from the Lesser Doxology: "Gloria Patri et Filio et Spiritui Sancto. Sicut erat in principio et nunc, et in sæcula sæculorum. Amen." The Greater Doxology begins: "Gloria in excelsis Deo." "Doxology" is from two Greek words meaning "praise" and a "discourse."

3. Bring us not, Lord, very low: for Thou hast said, Come back again, ye sons of Adam.

4. A thousand years before Thine eyes are but as yesterday: and as a watch of the night which is come and gone.

5. The grass springs up in the morning: at evening-tide it shrivels up and dies.

6. So we fail in Thine anger: and in Thy wrath we are troubled.

7. Thou hast set our sins in Thy sight: and our round of days in the light of Thy countenance.

8. Come back, O Lord! how long: and be entreated for Thy servants.

9. In Thy morning we shall be filled with Thy mercy: we shall rejoice and be in pleasure all our days.

10. We shall be glad according to the days of our humiliation: and the years in which we have seen evil.

11. Look, O Lord, upon Thy servants and on Thy work: and direct their children.

12. And let the beauty of the Lord our God be upon us: and the work of our hands, establish Thou it.

Glory be to the Father, and to the Son: and to the Holy Ghost.

As it was in the beginning, is now, and ever shall be: world without end. Amen.

Softly and gently, dearly-ransomed soul[36],

 In my most loving arms I now enfold thee,

And, o'er the penal waters, as they roll,

 I poise thee, and I lower thee, and hold thee.

And carefully I dip thee in the lake[37],

 And thou, without a sob or a resistance,

Dost through the flood thy rapid passage take,

 Sinking deep, deeper into the dim distance.

---

[36] *"Softly and gently, dearly ransomed soul,*
In my most loving arms I now enfold thee," etc.

[37] In Dante's Vision of Purgatory (Canto I.) hell is spoken of as a "cruel sea," and the water surrounding the Island of Purgatory as the "better waves." The spirit of Gerontius is dropped into these "better waves" — "miglior acqua."

> "Per correr miglior acqua alza le vele
> Omai la navicella del mio ingegno
> Che lascia dietro a se *mar si crudele*."

> "O'er better waves to speed her rapid course,
> The light bark of my genius lifts her sail,
> Well pleased to leave so cruel sea behind."

— Cary's Translation.

Angels, to whom the willing task is given,

      Shall tend, and nurse, and lull thee, as thou liest;

And Masses on the earth, and prayers in heaven,

      Shall aid thee at the Throne of the Most Highest.

Farewell, but not for ever! brother dear,

      Be brave and patient on thy bed of sorrow;

Swiftly shall pass thy night of trial here,

      And I will come and wake thee on the morrow.

The Oratory.

January, 1865.

THE ETERNAL YEARS

BY Frederick William Faber, D.D.[38]

1

How shalt thou bear the Cross that now
So dread a weight appears?
Keep quietly to God, and think
Upon the Eternal Years.

2

Austerity is little help,
Although it somewhat cheers;
Thine oil of gladness is the thought
Of the Eternal Years.

3

Set hours and written rule are good,
Long prayer can lay our fears:
But it is better calm for thee
To count the Eternal Years.

4

Rites are as balm unto the eyes,
God's word unto the ears:
But He will have thee rather brood
Upon the Eternal Years.

---

[38] "It appears that Newman thinks so highly of that poem ["The Eternal Years"] that he asked to have it sung to him during his recent illness, and remarked: '"Lead, Kindly Light" are the words of one seeking the truth. "The Eternal Years" are those of one who has found it.'" — May, 1889, Grant Duff's *Notes from a Diary*.

5

Full many things are good for souls
   In proper times and spheres;
Thy present good is in the thought
   Of the Eternal Years.

6

Thy self-upbraiding is a snare,
   Though meekness it appears;
More humbling is it far for thee
   To face the Eternal Years.

7

Brave quiet is the thing for thee,
   Chiding thy scrupulous fears;
Learn to be real, from the thought
   Of the Eternal Years.

8

Bear gently, suffer like a child,
   Nor be ashamed of tears;
Kiss the sweet Cross, and in thy heart
   Sing of the Eternal Years.

9

Thy Cross is quite enough for thee,
   Though little it appears;
For there is hid in it the weight
   Of the Eternal Years.

10

And knowst thou not how bitterness
    An ailing spirit cheers?
Thy medicine is the strengthening thought
    Of the Eternal Years.

11

One Cross can sanctify a soul;
    Late saints and ancient seers
Were what they were, because they mused
    Upon the Eternal Years.

12

Pass not from flower to pretty flower;
    Time flies, and judgment nears;
Go! make thy honey from the thought
    Of the Eternal Years.

13

Death will have rainbows round it, seen
    Through calm contrition's tears,
If tranquil hope but trims her lamp
    At the Eternal Years.

14

Keep unconstrain'dly in this thought,
    Thy loves, hopes, smiles, and tears;
Such prison-house thine heart will make
    Free of the Eternal Years.

15

A single practice long sustained
    A soul to God endears:
This must be thine—to weigh the thought
    Of the Eternal Years.

16

He practises all virtue well,
    Who his own Cross reveres,
And lives in the familiar thought
    Of the Eternal Years.

Made in the USA
Monee, IL
19 January 2022

89290403R00049